PALEOTEMPESTOLOGY

BERTHA ISABEL CROMBET

C&R Press
Conscious & Responsible

1
Winnter Soup Bowl Chapbook
2018 5th Collection Selection 1 of 2 CB 9

All Rights Reserved

Printed in the United States of America

First Edition
1 2 3 4 5 6 7 8 9

Selections of up to two pages may be reproduced without permissions. To reproduce more than two pages of any one portion of this book write to C&R Press publishers John Gosslee and Andrew Sullivan

Cover Art by Max Rippon
Interior and cover design by C&R Press

Copyright ©2018 Bertha Isabel Crombet

ISBN - 978-1-936196-98-2

C&R Press
Conscious & Responsible
www.crpress.org

For special discounted bulk purchases, please contact:
C&R Press sales@crpress.org
Contact info@crpress.org to book events, readings and author signings.

PALEOTEMPESTOLOGY

Table of Contents

WAITING FOR HURRICANE IRMA / 5
ODE TO SEMEN / 6
THE LIBRARY / 8
BRAD COMES TO ME AFTER HIS DIVORCE / 9
DATING APP GOTHIC / 10
CLAIRVOYANCE / 13
ODE TO THE BLUE BUTTON-DOWN SHIRT I BOUGHT YOU / 14
YOU BRING OUT THE CUBAN IN ME / 16
FRANK O'HARA LOVE POEM / 19
THE TAKING / 21
EXPORT MARINE / 23
LOVE POEM / 25
UPON LEARNING MY MAN HAS SPENT FRIDAY NIGHT AT TOOTSIE'S / 26
RAILROAD CROSSING / 28
ONLY POEM FOR MICHAEL / 31
FIRST KISS / 33
SMILIN' BOB'S SMOKED FISH DIP / 34
ODE TO KISSING / 35
HOROSCOPE / 36

WAITING FOR HURRICANE IRMA

Confession: I asked for this. I wished for a fresh disaster
to eclipse my old one. I lay in bed,
red wine stains dappling my sheets,
drunk off hunger after not eating for a week,
and I said *Please God, let something more terrible come.
Something bigger than this pain. Anything. Anything.*
And God leaned back in his brown leather armchair,
holed and bursting with polyester foam like
cookie dough from a Pillsbury tube,
propped his long feet up on the coffee table
littered in newspapers, and mused
on all of my past ridiculousness:
the midnight bargaining before exams I failed
to study for, excuses, unmet promises of all I'd give up
(meat on Fridays, men, the word "fuck"),
all while maintaining my skepticism. *If you even exist,
I'd start every prayer, then do me this solid, will ya?*
He was like the year-round Santa Claus whose lap
I got to sit on as soon as I dropped to my knees.
The genie unleashed when I rubbed
the ensorcelled lamp, wrists cuffed in gold,
a prisoner of his own phenomenal cosmic power.
I had this coming. Forgive me. I wanted so badly to mourn
something new, so that devastation
would extinguish all the old ones. Even you.
And God knew I meant business,
that I was all gristle and pulped heart, wrong and wronged,
my eyes two rags wrung and hung
out to dry in the yard, so he said *Here comes the storm
of a lifetime. Here's the catastrophe you've been crossing
all your fingers and toes for.* And I said, *Thank you.*

ODE TO SEMEN

For years, you were the enemy:
fleet of myrmidons fighting
for their pleasure-starved king,
viscous elixir, dreaded ingredient,
dangerous as a life. I was afraid of you
at nine or ten, my mother warning
against getting too close to the older boys,
their treacherous densities, missiles aimed
at the mystery between my legs, my center red
as a bullseye. I must have been sixteen
when I discovered the truth about you,
everyone in class, nubile and stupid,
timidly engrossed in the captioned images—
scrotum, urethra, penis—
suddenly betrayed by the foreignness
of their own bodies. O, spidery translucence,
O, knot of newts, as blind and full of gender as
Tiresias, as slippery as the S.
I like to feel you ribboning
inside me. O, one hundred million
peacock feathers in flight, arrows flung
by one million skilled archers. O,
silver starlight lingering after a supernova,
misting off the tired blue-flamed core.
Once, you were evil. Once, you inspired
panicked prayers and disgust.
But then you came to me, disarmed,
offering yourself like a gift,
fire of my other's flesh,
and made it known how much you needed me,
the warm wet shelter of my being, to live.
Gray and milky and marbled, like horned Moses,
alarmed eyes, clutching a menu for morality—
you made him by making his maker,

and his maker before him.
I owe you everything.

THE LIBRARY

The library smells like you,
like your clothes, like your bed and whole home—
old, deep, well-lived—and, for a moment,
I am inside you as I am inside it.
How peripatetic!
Me inside you, taking the shape and name
of all your stunning viscera,
the spines of the books gleaming
like slippery spleens, empurpled and intimate.
I'd travel the length of your flank
and settle in some fertile hollow between the ribs,
only to be created again from the fine bone, begotten,
this time better, more curious, more agile, even,
as I climbed through your eyes,
green and gray
like jade that has been splintered by lightning,
and finally up to your succulent brain, nibbling
on tangy morsels of memory,
feasting on them like a corpulent king,
your greasy dreams dripping down to my elbows.
Hungry—hungry—greedy—greedy!
Satisfied, I'd spelunk down to the middle of your middle,
right between those two great pink shelves of breath,
and ride the exhale out of you
like a skilled almond-skinned surfer.
Wouldn't you like to hear my report,
how I swallowed to learn you before I knew you?
Wouldn't you like me to tell you everything?

BRAD COMES TO ME AFTER HIS DIVORCE
After Kiki Petrosino

Your hair's so long, he says. *Has it always been this long?*
Of course not. I don't know why he asks. I haven't cut my hair
in two years. Most days it feels like an entity I am attached to,
a star my head orbits, followed by the satellites of my limbs:
one arm Phobos, one arm Deimos, my entire body a diorama
of our coy solar system, anchored firmly in the universe
by unspooled black curls. *We're not here to talk about me,* I reply.
He smirks, reaching over to pour me another glass of Glenlivet.
He pours himself another, too. Whiskey is the saddest spirit,
the most forlorn. He tilts his head back and gulps it down.
Everything about him is thinned and gray,
like watching sleet plummet diagonally through a wet window,
or a dulled needle in a wastebasket, or the shadows
between black and white in old Polaroids.
A sputter of sunbeam catches his face and it is a strained
rendition of the posters and ad campaigns,
rugged Tristan and doomed Achilles,
of the larger-than-life billboards that loomed over the city
like angels on time-out. *Tell me what you're thinking,* he says,
leaning forward with both elbows propped on the counter.
I'm thinking: there's no mystery to grief, only nuance.
Four months ago, when my love left, it felt like I was devouring
my own heart, all those toothsome chambers and valves,
sticky sweet coagulations of regret. But look at me now—
my pain metabolized. Complete. I know there are disparities:
decades, diamonds, children. But the resolution is the same:
everything, from now on, without them, that's all. I tell him this.

DATING APP GOTHIC

You make a Tinder profile. You make an OKCupid profile. You make a Match.com profile.

You swipe right on Kyle and agree to meet at a popular brunch spot.
You get there early so you can have a drink to take the edge off.
Eight mimosas later, your date shows up: he's a large Filipino man named Oscar.
He orders a mimosa and compliments your feet,
    how slender they are, your hot pink pedicure.
Where is Kyle?

You make a Bumble profile. You make a Hinge profile. You make a Plenty of Fish profile.

Swiping through Bumble, you stumble upon Brian.
Yes—he's the one.
You send him a message asking him his top three preferred pizza toppings.
Pineapple is number two.
You unmatch him.

You make a Zoosk profile. The earth is a small blue mistake.

You match with Nick on Tinder.
You both enjoy tacos, kayaking, and country music.
You're both fire signs.
He's 6'4", an executive chef, says he has a weakness for bangs and Cuban girls—
    you're perfect for one another!
Neither of you sends a message.

Is Kyle not coming?

Rob is from Baltimore.
He just moved here for work.
He wants to fuck you in the ass.

On your Hinge date with Troy, you mention how funny it is that you both enjoy tapas.
    Troy's face darkens.
    "I don't like tapas," he says. *"I hate tapas."*
You've confused Troy for Carlos. Carlos likes tapas. Or was it Lucas? Or Marc?
    Nobody loves you.

Eric has five pictures holding up the same fish.
You are sure he's trapped in a Groundhog Day scenario,
    forced to relive the same events over and over,
    confronted with all of his choices ad infinitum.
You swipe right.

You swipe and swipe until your phone dies,
    until every living thing around you dies,
    until there is nothing but the void,
    dark and desolate and complete,
    until there is only Oscar.

On Plenty of Fish, a 62-year old man in Istanbul asks for your hand in marriage.
    I could be happy, you think. *I could be happy.*

On OKCupid, Zach messages you asking for pictures of your feet.
    Close-ups, he writes. *None of that from-across-the-room bullshit.*

You swipe left on Greg.

He's wearing hats in all his pictures; you assume he's balding and insecure.

A few days later, Greg shows up again. You swipe left.

Soon after, he shows up yet again, and, again, you swipe left.

The fourth time, you notice as his face begins to change in the pictures,

    becomes distorted, his smile twisting into a menacing grimace.

Greg will not be ignored.

Adam is covered in tattoos, did a five-year stint in prison for manslaughter,

    texts you every night at 11:01 PM saying: *"send me a pic lol."*

You're in love with him.

You pause to read Ian's Match bio. It says:

    "In your early twenties, you used to be attractive. You used to have men lined up around the corner.

    You used to have a man who loved you—truly loved you. But you let him go.

    You wanted to keep riding the cock carousel, thinking you could find something better.

    Now you're in your thirties and men don't look at you the same way. Now, you are all alone.

    Now, all you have is me."

You send him a wink.

Kyle never shows.

Oscar is your boyfriend now.

As it turns out—he's the one.

CLAIRVOYANCE

In a lightning bolt glimpse of the future,
I see you, the still slender slab of your torso
twisting out of frayed denim shorts, so avuncular now.
You've been working in the yard, collecting fallen branches
after a summer storm. The sweat has condensed
in your eyelashes like morning dew and you reek
of something wild. Upstairs, our two or three or
four children are perfect and soft and loved.
You kiss the back of my legs, stopping to admire
the delicate, nameless place behind the knees.
I kiss your hands, stopping to admire
the delicate, nameless place between the knuckles.
In the kitchen, a tea kettle loses its temper.
In the garden, a ripe tomato falls on wet earth.

ODE TO THE BLUE BUTTON-DOWN SHIRT I BOUGHT YOU

It wasn't exactly blue, or it wasn't *just* blue,
it was aquamarine or celeste, cerulean
leaning toward cyan,
an XXL and 50% off at TJ Maxx.
There are a lot of Xs in this poem,
including you. But I loved you once,
so I bought it for you, that linen-cotton blend
almost-blue shirt. It had long sleeves,
which I imagine you would've rolled up,
ink-black wolf howling
at the hinged moon of your elbow,
but it seemed breathy,
light, perfect for summer.

You were still adjusting to Miami,
City Founded Inside
a Flared Nostril, every seatbelt buckle
a branding iron, even the rain
slowing in its descent
like nervous spelunkers. Nothing
like Baltimore, its indigenous unkindness
of ravens, their black shadows singing
the white alien earth.

But it's blue that reminds me of you—
frog-spleen-Windex-bottle-blueish-shirt-
blue. What have you done with it?
Is it collecting dust in your closet,
or at the bottom of a laundry heap,
or hanging at a Goodwill
beside vintage leather and acid wash denim?
Or worse: is it out in the world—

collar kissing your clavicle,
sheer linen billowing your flank,
a new prop in all your most
compelling auditions for love?

YOU BRING OUT THE CUBAN IN ME
After Sandra Cisneros

You bring out the Cuban in me,
the original red, white, and blue in me,
the *guajira* in me, the *¡Ay, papi!* in me,
the converted heathen,
the raw sugarcane nucleus,
the elusive *ñ* in me.

You bring out the superstitious in me,
the sacrificial lust in me,
the mystic and ritualistic in me.
Eleguá, Obatalá, Yemayá, Changó, Ochún, and I
drunk off palm wine,
ululating in Yoruba,
bleeding goats bleating.

The black pulp of my heart is yours.

You bring out the religious in me, the pious in me,
the Catholic fear of God in me.
Ten *Padre Nuestros* on two bruised knees
and the sting of a Sister's holy discipline.

I would fashion an altar in my armoire
out of rose quartz and coral, candles and rosary beads.
I would crawl from Oriente to El Rincon, repenting.

For you.

You bring out the José María Heredia in me.
José Martí's heroic sensibility in me.
La Niña de Guatemala in me.
The white rose I would cultivate

for a friend as well as an enemy.

Te quiero en junio como en enero, mi amor.

You bring out the love of Russia in me.
I am as barren as the Siberian wilderness
without the question of your pink tongue mystery.
I want you bad like a missile crisis.
I want you like nuclear war.

You invoke the immunity to caffeine in me.
The salsa, merengue,
and every other delicious dish
that doubles as a dance, in me.
The Celia Cruz *azucar*.
The güiro fever and drum delirium.
The maid, the cook, the slave in chains,
the makeshift raft for ninety miles at sea.

I want you like a Sunday slaughter.
Whole pig roasting on a spit,
crispy skin and flesh so fresh
I can still taste death.

This love isn't kosher, honey.
This love isn't squeamish.
This love walks around wielding a machete.

You bring out the dirty in me, the *chusma* in me,
The *¡Oye, que bolá?* and *¡Tremenda loca!* in me,
the *Don't fuck with me, that's my man!* in me,
the Great Hialean Commandment in me:
Thou shalt hold my hoops while I fight any bitch who covets
thee.

Anthem, *patria*, and plague.

I want to ravage you like a scourge of mosquitoes.
I want to stir you into my coffee, black and sweet.
I want to sing your name with my hand over my heart,
the flag billowing in the wind like a palm tree.

FRANK O'HARA LOVE POEM

Sharing an umbrella with you is the best part of rain:
the blue undulating pulse of the nimbostratus,
plump beads ricocheting off our nylon dome
as we scurry across a gleaming parking lot.

Best because we have to huddle close together
like a parliament of owls would,
prior to voting "yes" or "no" on passing a new law,
and considering our proximity, I know now
you smell like sweet linens and hot leather,
and upon further inspection, it becomes apparent to me
your skin is the color of perfectly creamed coffee,

except for the tattooed bits,
which you don't regret yet, but might,
once a native speaker of Sanskrit finally confirms
that the ink on your remarkable ribcage
does not read as an ancient protection prayer at all
but instead, as a recipe for coconut curry,
which is delicious and at least
I'd never have to go thumbing through a cookbook
when I could just thumb
the ridges and hollows of your bones
to know exactly how much coriander to add,

that is
if I understood Sanskrit,
that is if skin could swell into braille to instruct,
"Touch me here
                    and there,"

that is if either of us were blind
and needed the extra sensory stimulation,

but thank goodness we both have 20/20
and are able to see the sun emerge after the storm
(from which we'd sought shelter),
saturating the slick streets with the same kind of light
I imagine would flood Egyptian tombs
right before they were sealed shut
until some hot shot archeologist dressed like Indiana Jones
discovered the embalmed bodies
in their golden sarcophagi a thousand years later,
only to have them jettisoned to the Field Museum,
where you and I could finally gaze upon
their gorgeous gaunt brainless heads together.

And I am also particularly grateful
that both our eyes are blaring tantalum bulbs,
particularly yours because they are enormous and expressive,
particularly because they strip me of all sense and wit,
particularly because they ignite in me
the full spectrum of human emotion to such a degree that I feel
as if I might dissolve into a pillar of salt like Lot's wife,
or plunge backwards into the underworld like Eurydice,
or tie myself to a chestnut tree like José Arcadio Buendía
to vanquish the shiver of madness
when you look at me or when you don't look at me.

THE TAKING

She must have been petrified,
the possessed earth split across
that field of cypress and narcissus,
the crimson blossoms crumbling into the cleft
as he rose through it, Mister Death,
long fringe epaulettes hinged
on the black crescents of his shoulders,
his cloak and cape billowing behind him
like a wet, breathing shadow,
his platinum pupils coiling
to pinpricks in the sunlight
as he lowered his face to look at her,
still on her knees, clutching a fistful of white petals.

It was the first time he had ever left home,
his impenetrable bunker of souls,
where he had holed himself in
like an immortal general,
so protective of his dead army—
stubbornly so as they were already dead
and beyond protection, beyond tenderness—
weaponed only with sighs
and a thirsty impatient wandering—
down corridors, in and out of narrow rooms,
like the bright blood that rushes
with no more than animal luck
through arterial passages towards memory—
that their restless deadness
left no time for a life.

But he wanted her, heart rattling hot.

He pulled her onto his horse and under they plunged,

the earth sealing above them like a lacquered wound.

The first color to go was blue.

She was silent during their descent,
reluctant to touch him at first and then
gripping her arms tightly around him,
fingering the hollows between each of his ribs
to turn him more human, at least in thought,
his center still as cold as an old star.
They plummeted for an hour, through clouds that hung
like white fangs in the mouth of a wolf
who was devouring them whole.
But there was no pain, only a gradual darkening within,
as if someone had draped sheets of cotton
over all the mirrors inside her.
No light. No questions.

And when they finally arrived at the gates—
his ferocious dog suddenly gentle
beneath the weight of the dark man's hand,
her once strawberry hair silvering at the ends,
the horse's tired hind muscles prominent and twisting
beneath his obsidian coat like a storm of fists—
she heard him speak for the first time,
his voice like a gavel, guttering through the palace.
"*Welcome home,*" he said.

EXPORT MARINE

Who made you this way?
Was it your mom's second boyfriend
the summer of your 13th birthday?
The John who pressed a hand on your chest
to shove you out of the trailer
as he crumbled
Sudafed tablets over an open flame,
the orange globs of phenylephrine
clotting in the pot like honeycomb?
Or your daddy, who left a few years before that?
You had his name. You were a Joshua and
a William, too. You had his eyes,
blue as the blade of a scythe slicing
into a field of wild irises.
The rancor deepened and lengthened inside you
like the limbs of a river. Meanwhile,
I was learning how not to swim.
I was licking mayonnaise out of a blender.
I was watching my parents kiss
through a termite hole
in their bedroom door. It was a third-world or
it was developing or it was a cockroach
emerging from beneath a pile
of plastic time-torn toys.
Then, you traded Baltimore for Djibouti
and drank your own yellowed sweat—
black lava, limestone tornadoes, wild flamingoes
penduling their beaks into bloodied salt—
then, Miami, then: me.
And when you asked
how I came to America,
I told you what I tell everyone, I said,
I built a raft myself out of pork cracklings

*and red handkerchiefs, tamarind husks
and the mysterious innards
of the maraca, glued together by the same sticky stuff
the soul is made of.
Whose soul?* You asked.
I took a breath.

LOVE POEM
For Sharon Olds and George R.R. Martin

It was your idea to pour Pepto-Bismol
into the same shot glass that had been brimming with
hot tequila only moments earlier.
Reluctantly, I tipped it into me and felt the pink goo fill me
like all the other pink goo that fills me, so intimate.
It wasn't until I forced it all down
that you thought to check the expiration date on the bottle:
January 2014, three years ago,
back before the Cubs could ever dream
to win another World Series, and you were still living
in West Palm Beach with all the snowbirds and active seniors,
the alarm of old jangling bones during their early morning aerobics,
before we watched the season six finale of *Game of Thrones*
on my couch, in a crown of empty pizza boxes,
our bodies tangled and sticky—it was June—
your Blackwater Bay tenderly thumbing my Dragonstone,
my Narrow Sea warm between your Essos and Westeros,
our Iron Islands intertwined, tense and sensitive as a wish,
before I even knew you were a person in the world—real!
So, you poured yourself one too.

UPON LEARNING MY MAN HAS SPENT FRIDAY NIGHT AT TOOTSIE'S

At first, I'm seething. For years,
I've been trying to dodge recruitment
into that militant race of women
who live to serve
as border patrol for their men,
armed in "no's" and buttoned up
in sheeny blue,
bedraggled by medals on their lapels
that brag of all they've never let their lovers do.
I've tried to be *cool*. I've tried to be
chill. But God,
I am so fucking riled up,
thinking about those bubblegum bodies
causing friction in his Levi's,
a set of supple nipples
stroking the sides of his face,
settling for a moment
in the deep ridges of his dimples,
as a single bead of sweat
glimmers down her pinked breasts,
taut skin globed over saline,
and hooks onto his lip.
What did she taste like? I want to ask,
What did you see when you peered
inside her, her silo of glittering honeyed flesh?
I want to climb up on that stage
and dance beside her, my new twin,
nude as the day we emerged empurpled
from that same petaled place
where men in the champagne rooms
spend entire paychecks to re-enter.
I want to arrange for VIP passes

for all his buddies—from work,
from the Marines, the ones he spent his days
chewing bluegrass with and trekking through
the wet jungle with, knee deep in blood mud.
I want to line them up and bend over.
I want them to see, and him to see them seeing,
the greasy neon narrowing into the vertex
between my legs like the X on a treasure map.
Let me show you.
Let me show you how a woman forgives.

RAILROAD CROSSING

I'm sitting in the car
and all the birds are perfectly perched
on telephone wires, still
as winged clothespins.
The boxcars begin hissing along
like the terrific pulse of a slumbering animal,
waking—waking—awake.
I'm on the way to class and I know
where you are: idling on the couch
that reeks of sweat and perfume,
nestled between those two fat cats
whose names I always confused,
because they were identical,
both so ashen and striped
along all the same furred hinges.
Sisters. Twins.

The sun must look liquid in your sky,
as it does in mine,
like an exquisite piece
of hand-blown glass, cooling.
I wonder if you're still wearing
your black leather jacket
with the red and white stripes on the sleeves
and ampersanding down
those feral roads on your motorcycle.
I think about the patch of yellow hair
that clung to the nape of your neck,
tenderly peeking
from beneath your helmet,
the way it fanned in the fast fecund wind
as innocent as Iowa.

I remember your hands
tightening on the handlebars
as we drove into Waldo.
Abandoned for a century,
the train's red caboose like the lone survivor
of a plague, ancient and sinister.
I think of the crumbling mural
depicting Old Waldo,
wagons and girdled women,
gentleman in tops hats—all faceless.
No eyes. No mouths.

The streets are chatoyant
from this afternoon's storm,
and I think about the two slender glasses
from your grandparents' wedding,
which I broke while drunkenly washing dishes—
forgive me. I went to grab a drink
with a Republican last week,
just to spite myself,
now that happiness is off the table.
We went to the rooftop bar
on the 40th floor of the East Hotel.
He was ex-military, Christian,
so unlike you. *Push
him off*, I thought. *Push him off.*

But I knew something inside him
was ripe with pain, too,
and, anyway, the garden was enclosed
in a perimeter of tall plexiglass,
pulling every rogue glint from around us—
the neon, the gleam of windows,
the greasy shimmer of the river—
to the center where we stood by the bar,

a prism of emotion. So, I let him live.

That same night, I had a dream
about your eyes: green and gelatinous,
they were displayed in a jar
at a museum of curiosities
alongside taxidermic wildcats and wax people,
all visibly stunned to be as dead
as they were. I took it to mean
that you were dead, too,
and woke up out of breath, my throat raw
from shouting your name
through the synapses of the story,
each one like a door to a room
you had just left.

ONLY POEM FOR MICHAEL

I was just remembering you, and that night
we sat sozzled off vanilla beer at 2 AM
by the railroad tracks.
You crooned to me on the ukulele
and I yawped something ugsome in reply
to keep your ears on their toes,
the susurrus of hamburger wrappers
joggled in the wind beneath the train,
the hiss and clamor of it—like music, too.

A parade of passersby emerged from their miasmas
of smoke and booze to applaud
our little lollapalooza,
and then continued to stumble on
into that nebulous night,
stray beams of light sputtering through
the dollop of cumulus above us,
the moon, an old engine in the sky.

Which made me think of
that Friday in September
when we cooked dinner at your place.
Tilapia, submerged in egg wash
and smothered in flour.
Then, lemon juice, olive oil,
and crescents of white garlic,
glinting like slick jewels.
Finally, too toothsome rice
and a bottle of Fetzer, on sale for $6.99.

We ate in absolute darkness,
save for the dubious glimmer of a weary candle,
and cleaned our plates

the way obedient children do.
After the wine, you played the drums for me
until your entire body was glazed with sweat,
plump beads of it dissolving
in the warmth of your eyelashes like cotton candy,
the smell of it misting off your skin like lemon zest,
and later, your tongue—like licorice.

For dessert, now, I savor this memory.

FIRST KISS
A Golden Shovel

"I knew I could never live apart from them again,
the strange race with their massive bloodied hooves."
—from "Infinite Bliss" by Sharon Olds

It was the end of December, and you had a cold, but I
had never kissed a mouth like yours, pink as fresh tuna, so I knew
nothing on Earth could deter me and I
kissed you, your mouth a sweet pharmacy. I could
taste the menthol and ginger, and the raw perfume of the throat
    never
fawned over in poems, coated in a sour film like something that
    would not live,
that could not. When we finally pulled our mouths apart,
our bodies tensed in each other's arms from
residual wanting, both the want of wanting to leave them
and not, to run the enormous errand of slicing oneself open
    again—
the heart, gnarled like chewed fruit—or the
alternative: to pack it gingerly into a box, for storage in one's own
    strange
pharmacy. What is it with us? This race
of lonely unwinged creatures, all gristle and membrane, each with
their own salts and perfumes, their
own pharmacies of pain and delight, those massive
chambers? I can only tell you what I did, what I do: I take the
    bloodied
bulb and keep slicing, the organ split like a dozen red hooves.

SMILIN' BOB'S SMOKED FISH DIP

reminds me of something that never happened,
because you never came and we never did meet,
and you're still in Columbia or Denver or
San Diego, maybe,
reconnecting with your ex-wife—
lithe and fey-eyed
like a siren responsible for a shipwreck—
but the briny amberjack spread on a tortilla chip
always sparks a mysterious vision
of us lolling on a hammock in Key West,
licking the stubborn crumbs off our fingers
beneath an arbor of ginger blooms—
our bodies, two full-bellied exclamations
of impossible smoky fishy delight.

ODE TO KISSING

It's like waking from an eternal sleep,
like a pilgrim's palms in prayer,
like surrender, like forgiveness,
like the hinge of a door swinging
between thirst and satiety,
like a sparrow feeding its hatchlings,
like the Big Bang, like betrayal.
Kissing is a respite from loneliness,
Rhett and Scarlett
twisting to fit each other,
kissing is a tumult of tongues, a tryst of teeth,
kissing is like building a house out of mouths,
like a knock on the door: open up,
like a hungry dinner guest:
"Yes, more please,"
like two dogs sharing a plate of spaghetti,
like a Gustav Klimt painting,
both lovers draped in a yellow cloak,
eyes closed and knuckles white,
like a jury willing to convict
on a thousand counts of being delicious
in the first degree,
like ripe fruit, engorged with sweetness,
like a meteor hurling toward Earth,
reckless and exciting,
every mouth unable to decide
whether to pray or to kiss.

HOROSCOPE

Happy Birthday, dearest Sagittarius.
Some days you feel like the light
dribbling between the fingers of a hand
shielding a face from the sun, don't you?
But it's not your face, it's his. And they're not your hands.
Be mindful of your health. You will only live until
the knobs of your father's ankles stop turning.
Eat more carrots. Get some rest.
How long has it been since you slept?
How long has it been since you
stopped grinding your molars down to a fine powder
like an elephant in mourning,
something to be mixed in with oil paints,
to add texture to a blossoming cypress?
Sagittarius, your friends and family need you
to count to a hundred and then go find them.
There they are, in the blue cupboards, glinting.
There they are in the whites of the pianos. There they go.
You're twenty-seven and your thighs are lacquered
in tight denim, your heeled brown boots slam
through a loud downtown street,
even the stars are silenced by the whirring fluorescence
like seeds budding just below the earth,
those bright fruits of night. Where are you going
drenched in the woolen shadow of the past? Sagittarius,
this Thursday the moon will be so full you will mistake it
for a womb, like in that dream you have
where you turn sideways in a mirror only to discover
you're pregnant, and you go find him at a party to tell him,
combing the crowd for the diamond hollow
of his throat, and you find him,
and you're dressed all in ivory and he's dressed all in ivory,
and you tell him, but all he does is chuckle and say,

"I've never seen you before in my life,"
the creases of his eyes dancing like
a gypsy's fingers over a crystal ball.
And you eat them all up, your babies, raw and unborn,
because you don't know what else to do,
their tender sweet pink bellies bursting in your mouth,
and you're so full that
you mistake yourself for the moon.

C&R PRESS CHAPBOOKS

C&R Press hosts two chapbook selection periods from June to September and November to March coupled with a reading in New York City each year. The Winter Soup Bowl and Summer Tide Pool Chapbook Series are open to new and established writers in poetry, fiction, essay and other creative writing.

2018 Winter Soup Bowl
Paleotemptestology by Bertha Crombet
White Boys from Hell by Jeffrey Skinner

2017 Summer Tide Pool
Atypical Cells of Undetermined Significance by Brenna Womer

2017 Winter Soup Bowl
Heredity and Other Inventions by Sharona Muir
On Inaccuracy by Joe Manning

2016 Summer Tide Pool
Cuntstruck by Kate Northrop
Relief Map by Erin M. Bertram
Love Undefined by Jonathan Katz

2016 Winter Soup Bowl
Notes from the Negro Side of the Moon by Earl Braggs
A Hunger Called Music: A Verse History in Black Music by Meredith Nnoka

C&R PRESS TITLES

NONFICTION

Women in the Literary Landscape by Doris Weatherford, et al
Credo: An Anthology of Manifestos & Sourcebook for Creative Writing by Rita Banerjee and Diana Norma Szokolyai

FICTION

Made by Mary by Laura Catherine Brown
Ivy vs. Dogg by Brian Leung
While You Were Gone by Sybil Baker
Cloud Diary by Steve Mitchell
Spectrum by Martin Ott
That Man in Our Lives by Xu Xi

SHORT FICTION

Notes From the Mother Tongue by An Tran
The Protester Has Been Released by Janet Sarbanes

ESSAY AND CREATIVE NONFICTION

Immigration Essays by Sybil Baker
Je suis l'autre: Essays and Interrogations by Kristina Marie Darling
Death of Art by Chris Campanioni

POETRY

Lessons in Camoflauge by Martin Ott
Dark Horse by Kristina Marie Darling
All My Heroes are Broke by Ariel Francisco
Holdfast by Christian Anton Gerard
Ex Domestica by E.G. Cunningham
Like Lesser Gods by Bruce McEver
Notes from the Negro Side of the Moon by Earl Braggs
Imagine Not Drowning by Kelli Allen
Notes to the Beloved by Michelle Bitting
Free Boat: Collected Lies and Love Poems by John Reed
Les Fauves by Barbara Crooker
Tall as You are Tall Between Them by Annie Christain
The Couple Who Fell to Earth by Michelle Bitting
Notes to the Beloved by Michelle Bitting

www.ingramcontent.com/pod-product-compliance
Lightning Source LLC
Chambersburg PA
CBHW032105040426
42449CB00007B/1191